Greetings, aircraft carriers!

MARVELS VEHICLES 35

AIRCRAFT CARRIERS

GRACE BELTOWSKI

CREATIVE EDUCATION | CREATIVE PAPERBACKS

I MIGHT BE BIG, BUT I CAN MOVE!

table of contents

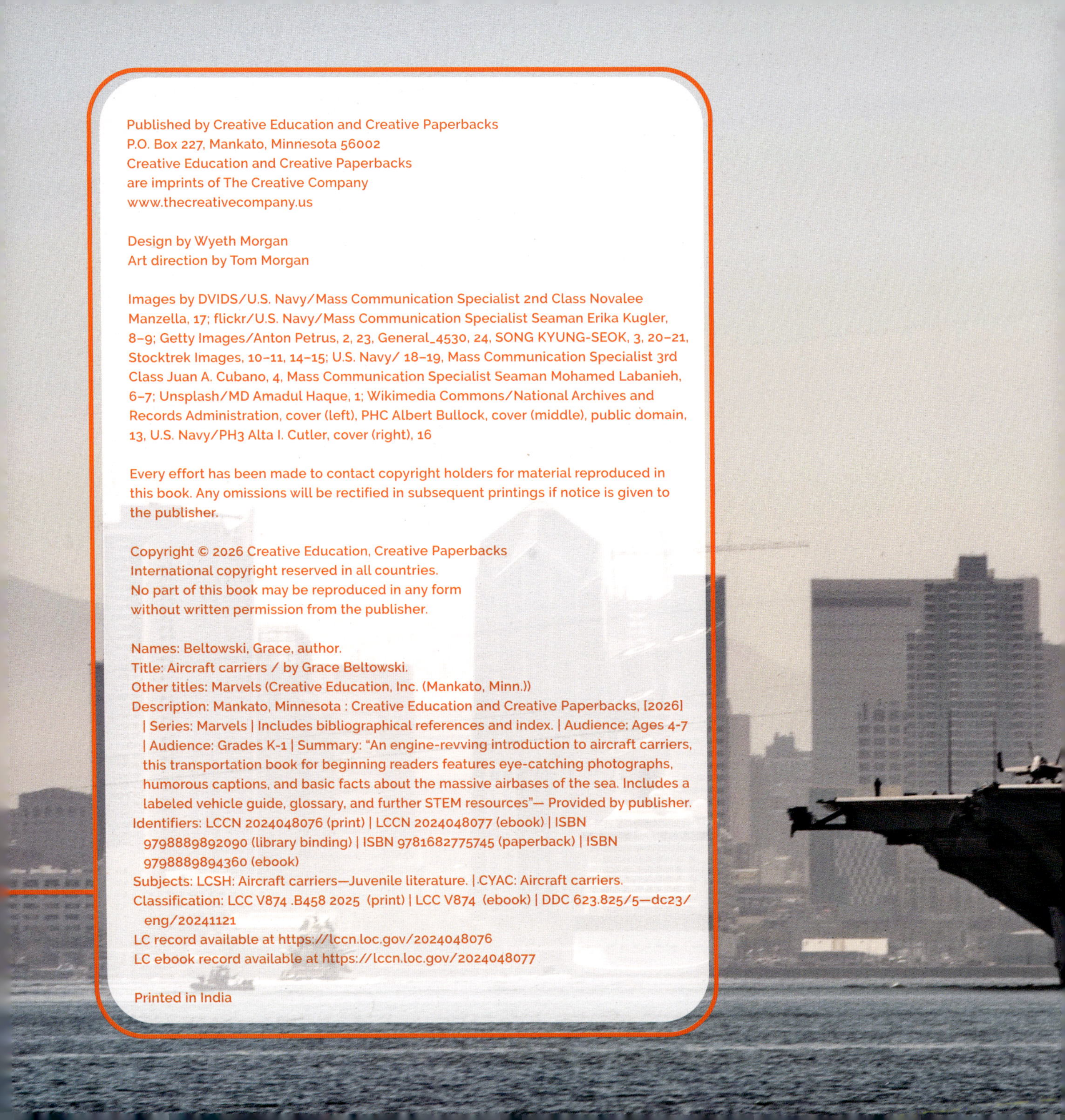

Published by Creative Education and Creative Paperbacks
P.O. Box 227, Mankato, Minnesota 56002
Creative Education and Creative Paperbacks
are imprints of The Creative Company
www.thecreativecompany.us

Design by Wyeth Morgan
Art direction by Tom Morgan

Images by DVIDS/U.S. Navy/Mass Communication Specialist 2nd Class Novalee Manzella, 17; flickr/U.S. Navy/Mass Communication Specialist Seaman Erika Kugler, 8–9; Getty Images/Anton Petrus, 2, 23, General_4530, 24, SONG KYUNG-SEOK, 3, 20–21, Stocktrek Images, 10–11, 14–15; U.S. Navy/ 18–19, Mass Communication Specialist 3rd Class Juan A. Cubano, 4, Mass Communication Specialist Seaman Mohamed Labanieh, 6–7; Unsplash/MD Amadul Haque, 1; Wikimedia Commons/National Archives and Records Administration, cover (left), PHC Albert Bullock, cover (middle), public domain, 13, U.S. Navy/PH3 Alta I. Cutler, cover (right), 16

Names: Beltowski, Grace, author.
Title: Aircraft carriers / by Grace Beltowski.
Other titles: Marvels (Creative Education, Inc. (Mankato, Minn.))
Description: Mankato, Minnesota : Creative Education and Creative Paperbacks, [2026] | Series: Marvels | Includes bibliographical references and index. | Audience: Ages 4-7 | Audience: Grades K-1 | Summary: "An engine-revving introduction to aircraft carriers, this transportation book for beginning readers features eye-catching photographs, humorous captions, and basic facts about the massive airbases of the sea. Includes a labeled vehicle guide, glossary, and further STEM resources"— Provided by publisher.
Identifiers: LCCN 2024048076 (print) | LCCN 2024048077 (ebook) | ISBN 9798889892090 (library binding) | ISBN 9781682775745 (paperback) | ISBN 9798889894360 (ebook)
Subjects: LCSH: Aircraft carriers—Juvenile literature. | CYAC: Aircraft carriers.
Classification: LCC V874 .B458 2025 (print) | LCC V874 (ebook) | DDC 623.825/5—dc23/eng/20241121
LC record available at https://lccn.loc.gov/2024048076
LC ebook record available at https://lccn.loc.gov/2024048077

Printed in India

Aircraft carriers are big ships. They are huge ocean air bases.

I BET IT'S WARM UP THERE.

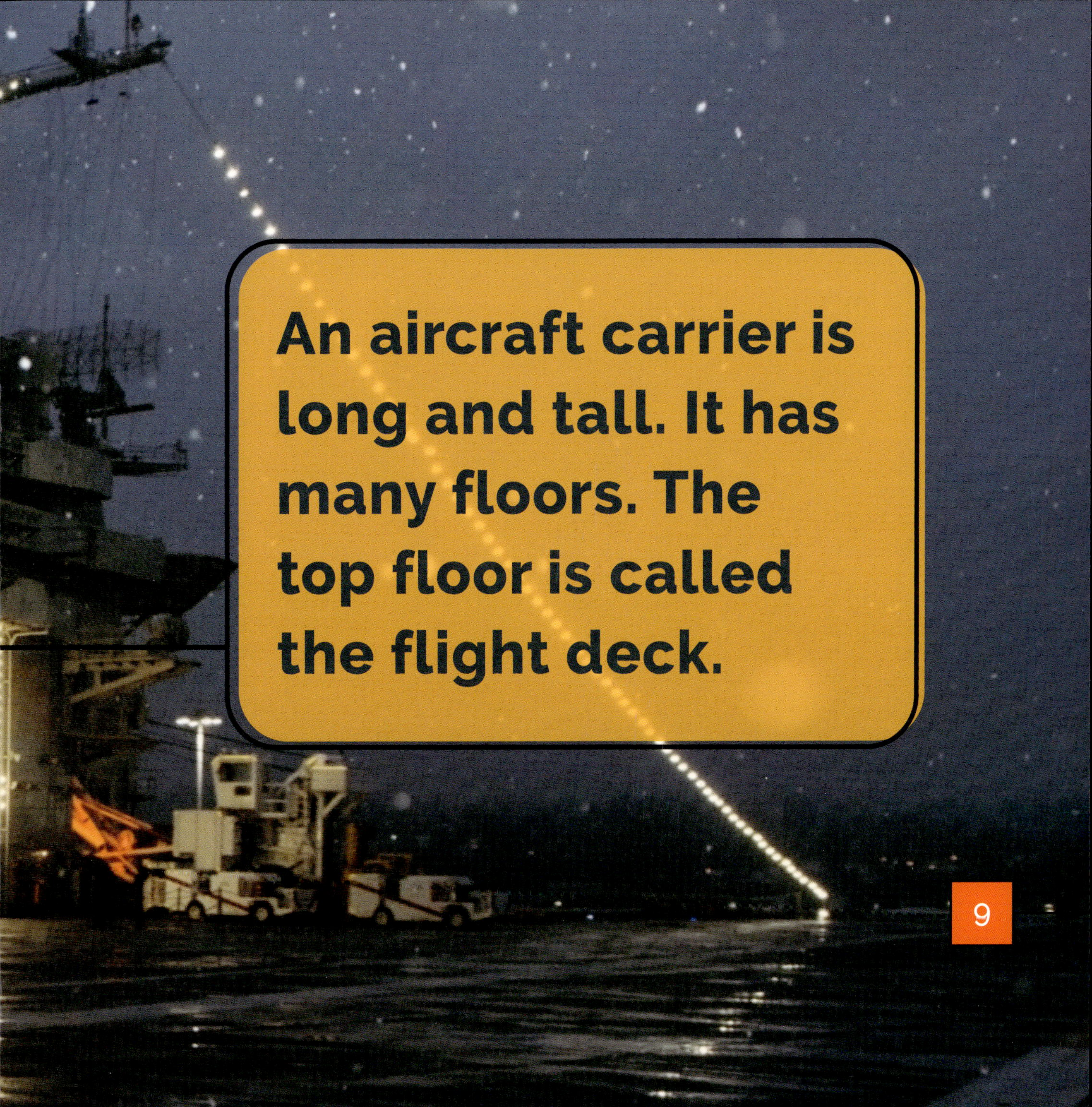

An aircraft carrier is long and tall. It has many floors. The top floor is called the flight deck.

An airplane speeds down a **runway**. It takes off. Look at it go!

MANY AIRPLANES TAKE OFF EACH DAY.

A captain controls the ship. Many workers help the airplanes take off and land.

MY NAME IS CAPTAIN RICK "POWDER" BURGESS!

SOME AIRCRAFT CARRIERS HOLD MORE THAN 100 AIRPLANES.

The airplane flies back to the ship. It lands safely on the runway.

Aircraft carriers have their own guns. They fight in battles. They protect the seas.

75

Farewell, aircraft carriers!

[Picture an Aircraft Carrier]

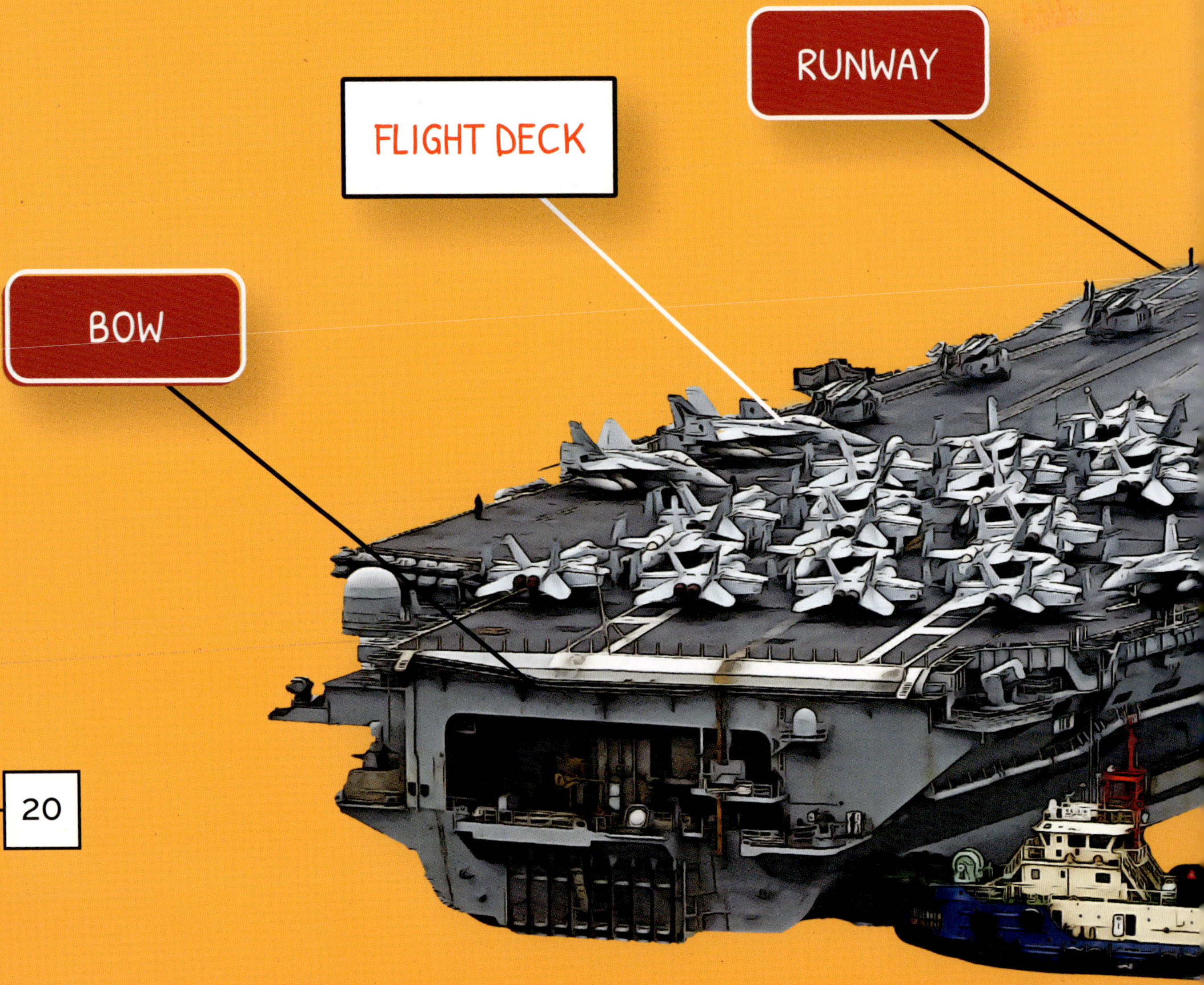

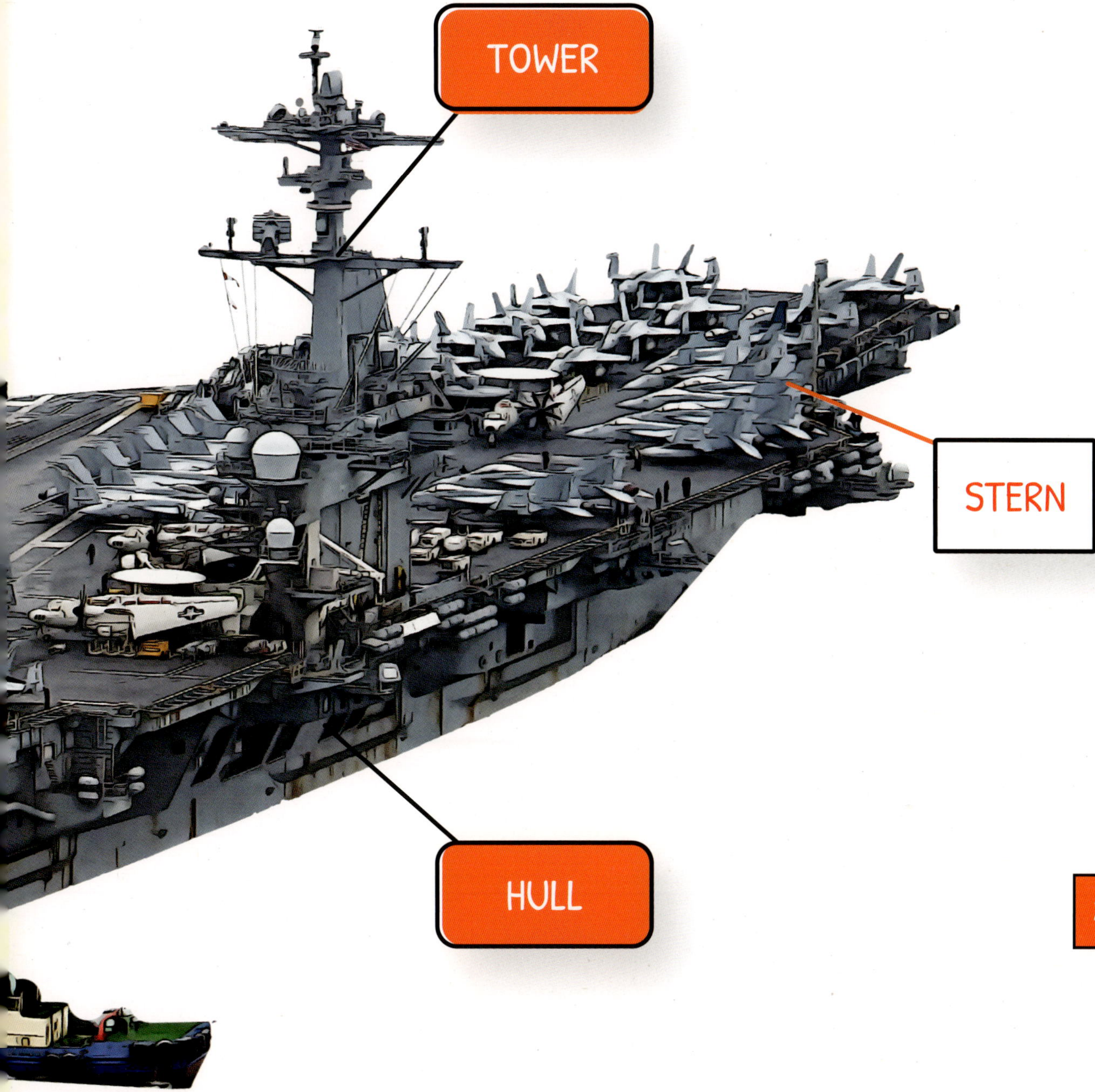
TOWER
STERN
HULL

WORDS TO KNOW

air base: a place where military airplanes come and go

battle: a fight between two armies or countries

runway: a strip of smooth ground where airplanes take off and land

READ MORE

Ransom, Candice. *How Aircraft Carriers Work*. Minneapolis: Lerner Publications, 2020.

Schuh, Mari. *Military Ships and Submarines*. North Mankato, Minn.: Pebble, 2023.

WEBSITES

Ducksters: World War II Aircraft Carriers
https://www.ducksters.com/history/world_war_ii/aircraft_carriers_in_ww2.php

Learn about how aircraft carriers were used during World War II.

Kiddle: Aircraft Carrier Facts for Kids
https://kids.kiddle.co/Aircraft_carrier

Read about the parts of an aircraft carrier and look at photos of different ships.

INDEX